40 minute
BIBLE STUDIES

W9-BOM-274

Breaking Free
from Fear

Kay Arthur

PRECEPT MINISTRIES INTERNATIONAL

WATERBROOK
PRESS

BREAKING FREE FROM FEAR
PUBLISHED BY WATERBROOK PRESS
12265 Oracle Boulevard, Suite 200
Colorado Springs, Colorado 80921

All Scripture quotations, unless otherwise indicated, are taken from the *New American Standard Bible®*. © Copyright The Lockman Foundation 1960, 1962, 1963, 1968, 1971, 1972, 1973, 1975, 1977, 1995, and Mark 4:40 from 1997. Used by permission. (www.Lockman .org) Scripture quotations marked (ESV) are taken from The Holy Bible, English Standard Version, copyright ©2001 by Crossway Bibles, a division of Good News Publishers. Used by permission. All rights reserved.

Italics in Scripture quotations reflect the author's added emphasis.

ISBN 978-0-307-72985-9
ISBN 978-0-307-72986-6 (electronic)

Cover design by Kristopher K. Orr

Published in the United States by WaterBrook Multnomah, an imprint of the Crown Publishing Group, a division of Random House Inc., New York.

WATERBROOK and its deer colophon are registered trademarks of Random House Inc.

Printed in the United States of America
2013

10 9 8 7 6 5 4 3

SPECIAL SALES
Most WaterBrook Multnomah books are available at special quantity discounts when purchased in bulk by corporations, organizations, and special-interest groups. Custom imprinting or excerpting can also be done to fit special needs. For information, please e-mail SpecialMarkets@WaterBrookMultnomah.com or call 1-800-603-7051.

CONTENTS

HOW TO USE THIS STUDY

This small-group study is for people who are interested in learning for themselves more about what the Bible says on various subjects, but who have only limited time to meet together. It's ideal, for example, for a lunch group at work, an early morning men's group, a young mothers' group meeting in a home, a Sunday-school class, or even family devotions. (It's also ideal for small groups that typically have longer meeting times—such as evening groups or Saturday morning groups—but want to devote only a portion of their time together to actual study, while reserving the rest for prayer, fellowship, or other activities.)

This book is designed so that all the group's participants will complete each lesson's study activities *at the same time.* Discussing your insights drawn from what God says about the subject reveals exciting, life-impacting truths.

Although it's a group study, you'll need a facilitator to lead the study and keep the discussion moving. (This person's function is *not* that of a lecturer or teacher. However, when this book is used in a Sunday-school class or similar setting, the teacher should feel free to lead more directly and to bring in other insights in addition to those provided in each week's lesson.)

If *you* are your group's facilitator, the leader, here are some helpful points for making your job easier:

- Go through the lesson and mark the text before you lead the group. This will give you increased familiarity with the material and will enable you to facilitate the group with greater ease. It may be easier for you to lead the group through the instructions for marking if you, as a leader, choose a specific color for each symbol you mark.

- As you lead the group, start at the beginning of the text and simply read it aloud in the order it appears in the lesson, including the "insight boxes," which appear throughout. Work through the lesson together, observing and discussing what you learn. As you read the Scripture verses, have the group say aloud the word they are marking in the text.

- The discussion questions are there simply to help you cover the material. As the class moves into the discussion, many times you will find that they will cover the questions on their own. Remember, the discussion questions are there to guide the group through the topic, not to squelch discussion.

- Remember how important it is for people to verbalize their answers and discoveries. This greatly strengthens their personal understanding of each week's lesson. Try to ensure that everyone has plenty of opportunity to contribute to each week's discussions.

- Keep the discussion moving. This may mean spending more time on some parts of the study than on others. If necessary, you should feel free to spread out a lesson over more than one session. However, remember that you don't want to slow the pace too much. It's much better to leave everyone "wanting more" than to have people dropping out because of declining interest.

- If the validity or accuracy of some of the answers seems questionable, you can gently and cheerfully remind the group to stay focused on the truth of the Scriptures. Your object is to learn what the Bible says, not to engage in human philosophy. Simply stick with the Scriptures and give God the opportunity to speak. His Word *is* truth (John 17:17)!

BREAKING FREE FROM FEAR

L ife is filled with all sorts of fears, isn't it? Fears of terrorism and natural disasters. Fears about the economy, the safety of loved ones, dreaded diagnoses. Fears of losing a job, a home, a relationship, our savings, our dreams, our independence, our health, our lives. We can find so many reasons to be fearful.

And in these days of instant news, we seem to hear continually about the latest disasters, calamities, and tragedies striking our world—a world that seems to be shrinking, bringing each dangerous development closer and closer to us.

How do we free ourselves from the grip of fear and the accompanying stress that takes a toll on our lives physically, emotionally, mentally? In this study you'll discover the answer—an answer that will enable you to walk in faith and freedom, no matter what circumstances loom in your life.

God has promised us that nothing would ever overtake us that we could not handle (1 Corinthians 10:13). Therefore He has a way of escape—and when you see it for yourself and, in faith, order your life accordingly, you'll find yourself able to break free from fear's bondage.

As you begin this study, why don't you take just a moment to tell God you are ready to hear what He says and ask Him to speak to you through His Word, the Bible.

Fear can be paralyzing, confusing, wreaking havoc in our body and mind. When it hits, the best thing you can do is ask the question Jesus asked of His disciples: "Why are you afraid?" That question is also a good place to begin our study.

OBSERVE

Let's look at the occasion that prompted the question. Using the gospel of Luke as our chronological timeline, we can know that this event took place near the end of Jesus' second year of public ministry. By this time, Jesus' disciples had seen Him perform all sorts of miracles, from healing the sick to raising the dead to feeding the multitude with a few loaves and fishes.

Leader: Read Mark 4:35–41 aloud. Have the group say aloud and...

- *underline all references to **the disciples**, indicated in this passage by the pronouns **them, they, we,** and **you.***
- *put a cross like this* † *over all references to **Jesus,** indicated in this passage by the pronouns **He** and **Him.***
- *draw a jagged circle around **afraid,** like this:*

MARK 4:35–41

35 On that day, when evening came, He said to them, "Let us go over to the other side."

36 Leaving the crowd, they took Him along with them in the boat, just as He was; and other boats were with Him.

37 And there arose a fierce gale of wind, and the waves were breaking over the boat so much that the boat was already filling up.

38 Jesus Himself was in the stern, asleep on the cushion; and they woke Him and said to Him, "Teacher, do You not care that we are perishing?"

39 And He got up and rebuked the wind and said to the sea, "Hush, be still." And the wind died down and it became perfectly calm.

40 And He said to them, "Why are you afraid? How is it that you have no faith?"

As you read the text, it's helpful to have the group say the key words aloud as they mark them. This way everyone will be sure they are marking every occurrence of the word, including any synonymous words or phrases. Do this throughout the study.

DISCUSS

• What were the disciples experiencing? What did they think was going to happen?

• Where was Jesus and what did He do? Describe what happened.

• From what you've just read, would you describe the emotion displayed by the disciples as normal—a natural response given the circumstances? Explain your answer.

• What point was Jesus making when He asked the disciples, *"Why are you afraid? How is it that you have no faith?"*

- How should they have responded in this stormy crisis, and why?

- What did you learn from marking the two occurrences of *afraid*? Or to put it another way, why did the disciples become "very much afraid" in verse 41?

- Which should be the greater fear: fear of the storm in which we might perish or fear of the One who has authority over the storm? Why?

- Now, what are some fears you or other Christians you know are dealing with?

- From what you've just read, what is the appropriate response to these fears?

41 They became very much afraid and said to one another, "Who then is this, that even the wind and the sea obey Him?"

MATTHEW 14:24–33

24 But the boat was already a long distance from the land, battered by the waves; for the wind was contrary.

25 And in the fourth watch of the night He came to them, walking on the sea.

26 When the disciples saw Him walking on the sea, they were terrified, and said, "It is a ghost!" And they cried out in fear.

27 But immediately Jesus spoke to them, saying, "Take courage, it is I; do not be afraid." "cheer"

28 Peter said to Him, "Lord, if it is You, command me to come to You on the water."

OBSERVE

Let's look at another rough night on the Sea of Galilee and see what we can learn about the *why* of our fear. Jesus had sent His disciples ahead in a boat while He went alone to the mountain near the sea to pray.

Leader: Read Matthew 14:24–33 aloud and have the group...

- *put a cross over every reference to **Jesus**, including synonyms and pronouns.*
- *underline the references to **Peter**, including pronouns.*
- *draw a jagged circle around any reference to **fear, being afraid, frightened**, or **terrified**.*

DISCUSS

- Describe the situation in general.

- For each place you marked a reference to fear, discuss the fear, its cause, and what you learned from it.

• What happened with Peter and Jesus?

• What, if anything, can be learned from the way Peter handled his fear?

• Look at the places where you marked the references to Jesus. What did you learn from—or about—Jesus that can help when fear hits you, when you're afraid or terrified? What did Jesus do and say? How did He handle Peter? *You are in need*

- practicle .

• What do you think it means "to take courage" (verse 27)? What does this look like in a person's life?

29 And He said, "Come!" And Peter got out of the boat, and walked on the water and came toward Jesus.

30 But seeing the wind, he became frightened, and beginning to sink, he cried out, "Lord, save me!"

31 Immediately Jesus stretched out His hand and took hold of him, and said to him, "You of little faith, why did you doubt?"

32 When they got into the boat, the wind stopped.

33 And those who were in the boat worshiped Him, saying, "You are certainly God's Son!"

PSALM 56:1–4, 8–13

¹ Be gracious to me,
O God, for man has
trampled upon me;
fighting all day long
he oppresses me.

² My foes have
trampled upon me
all day long, for they
are many who fight
proudly against me.

³ When I am afraid,
I will put my trust in
You.

⁴ In God, whose
word I praise, in God
I have put my trust; I
shall not be afraid.
What can mere man
do to me?…

⁸ You have taken
account of my wan-
derings; put my tears
in Your bottle. Are
they not in Your book?

OBSERVE

Life wasn't easy for David, the man
anointed by Samuel as the next king of
Israel. While attempting to escape from
jealous King Saul, who wanted to kill him,
David was seized by the Philistines in
Gath. David wrote Psalm 56 during this
difficult situation. Let's see what we can
learn from his words.

*Leader: Read Psalm 56:1–4, 8–13 and
have the group…*
- *underline every reference to **David**—
  every **me**, **I**, **my**.*
- *mark every reference to **God**, including
  pronouns, with a triangle:* △
- *draw a jagged circle around every reference to **being afraid**.*

DISCUSS

- First discuss David's situation, nothing
  else. Get the facts: What was David dealing with? How did he feel? Don't miss
  any aspect of this situation.

- Now, how did David handle these circumstances? (Remember David knew God had anointed him to be the next king.) What reasoning, what thinking shaped his response?

- What did you learn from David that you can use in times of fear? Be very specific.

- What did David know about God?

- What role, or part, did the Word of God have in this situation?

  grateful

- Do you know what David knew about God? Or are there aspects of what David wrote that you are not as certain about? Discuss them as a group.

- So bottom line, what have you learned that can help you personally when you are afraid, fearful?

9 Then my enemies will turn back in the day when I call; this I know, that God is for me.

10 In God, whose word I praise, in the LORD, whose word I praise,

11 In God I have put my trust, I shall not be afraid. What can man do to me?

12 Your vows are binding upon me, O God; I will render thank offerings to You.

13 For You have delivered my soul from death, indeed my feet from stumbling, so that I may walk before God in the light of the living.

WRAP IT UP

When we face life-threatening situations, fear is natural. We live in a body of flesh, which shrinks from pain, runs from death. Yet, in each of the situations we studied this week, we saw that fear was not to be entertained or allowed free rein. Rather fear was to be tamed—harnessed by faith. For the disciples, fear was tamed by remembering that Jesus was there—in the same boat or walking on water. He was in control of the storm and flattening the waves. He reminded His disciples of the choice between fear and faith. Faith conquers fear.

Then we looked at David, a man who confessed that he was oppressed, trampled on, shedding tears—afraid. Yet he recorded for posterity that "When I am afraid, I will put my trust in You" (Psalm 56:3). The future king didn't minimize his situation or deny his feelings; rather he described how he conquered fear's bondage: David put His trust in God. In doing so he declared, "I shall not be afraid" (verse 11). Man is merely man, while God is God—and "God is for me" (verse 9). His confident words are later echoed in the apostle Paul's divinely inspired words in Romans 8:31: "If God is for us, who is against us?"

So when fear comes, ask yourself, "Why am I afraid?"

Then decide whether you'll move forward in fear or in faith.

Fear can be provoked by circumstances, by things we see, or by words we hear. Fear is rooted in what we believe; it's a state of mind that can take a toll on our bodies and spirits.

Do you remember what David wrote in Psalm 56:3? "When I am afraid, I will put my trust in You." Do you remember what Jesus said to the disciples in the midst of the storm? "Why are you afraid? How is it that you have no faith?" (Mark 4:40). In both instances, when fear came it was to be replaced with trust in the Lord, with faith.

What is so incredible is that freedom from fear comes through the fear of the Lord! Such fear is demonstrated by our reverence, respect, awe, confidence, trust. Trust in who He is, in what He says, and in what He is able to do simply because He is God.

That is what this lesson is about: finding out more about God and His intentions toward you. Then you can decide whether your life will be ruled by circumstances or by the fear of the Lord.

OBSERVE

Leader: Read Proverbs 29:25 aloud. Have the group say and…

- *draw a jagged circle around **fear.***
- *mark **trusts** with a big* **T.**

PROVERBS 29:25

The fear of man brings a snare, but he who trusts in the LORD will be exalted.

DISCUSS

- What two states of mind are contrasted in this verse? And what is the result of each?

INSIGHT

The Hebrew word translated *trusts* in this verse expresses a sense of well-being and security that results from having something or someone in whom to place confidence.

Exalted carries the idea of being lifted up and, therefore, secure.

• From what you observed in the text, can the fear of man and trust in the Lord co-exist? Or is it an "either/or situation"? Explain your answer.

OBSERVE

If you are going to trust in the Lord, then you have to know Him—what He is like, what He is capable of, the power He has, the extent of His dominion, and what His intentions are toward you as an individual. While time and space do not permit a thorough search of the Word of God, let's look at a few key verses that will give you a deeper understanding of who He is.

Leader: *Read aloud Psalm 103:19; 89:14; Isaiah 14:24, 27; 45:5–7; and Jeremiah 33:2–3; 32:26–27.*
> • *Have the group say and mark all references to* **the Lord,** *including pronouns, with a triangle.*

DISCUSS

• Looking at the passages one by one, discuss what you learned about the Lord and how this knowledge of God would help you in specific situations that might bring fear.

PSALM 103:19

The LORD has established His throne in the heavens, and His sovereignty rules over all.

PSALM 89:14

Righteousness and justice are the foundation of Your throne; lovingkindness and truth go before You.

ISAIAH 14:24, 27

24 The LORD of hosts has sworn saying, "Surely, just as I have intended so it has happened, and just as I have planned so it will stand.…

27 "For the LORD of hosts has planned, and who can frustrate it? And as for His stretched-out hand, who can turn it back?"

Isaiah 45:5–7

⁵ I am the LORD, and there is no other; besides Me there is no God. I will gird you, though you have not known Me;

⁶ that men may know from the rising to the setting of the sun that there is no one besides Me. I am the LORD, and there is no other,

⁷ the One forming light and creating darkness, causing well-being and creating calamity; I am the LORD who does all these.

Jeremiah 33:2–3

² Thus says the LORD who made the earth, the LORD who formed it to establish it, the LORD is His name,

• How do the truths of Psalm 103:19 and Psalm 89:14 help you understand what Isaiah 45:7 tells you about the Lord?

• Now are you willing to embrace these truths? Although you may not fully understand them, do you believe that God is in authority over every circumstance you will ever face?

• Look again at Psalm 89:14. How does God wield His power? In other words, can He be trusted? Explain your answer.

3 "Call to Me and I will answer you, and I will tell you great and mighty things, which you do not know."

JEREMIAH 32:26–27

26 Then the word of the LORD came to Jeremiah, saying,

27 "Behold, I am the LORD, the God of all flesh; is anything too difficult for Me?"

OBSERVE

Now that we've briefly considered the breadth of God's power, let's narrow the focus to His relationship with you.

Leader: *Read aloud Psalm 139:13–17; Ephesians 1:3–5; 2:8–10; and Psalm 138:8.*
   • *Have the group say and underline every* ***me, my, I, us, you*** *that refers to us.*

PSALM 139:13–17

13 For You [*God*] formed my inward parts; You wove me in my mother's womb.

14 I will give thanks to You, for I am fearfully and wonderfully made; wonderful are Your works, and my soul knows it very well.

15 My frame was not hidden from You, when I was made in secret, and skillfully wrought in the depths of the earth;

16 Your eyes have seen my unformed substance; and in Your book were all written the days that were ordained for me, when as yet there was not one of the them.

17 How precious also are Your thoughts to me, O God! How vast is the sum of them!

EPHESIANS 1:3–5

3 Blessed be the God and Father of our Lord Jesus Christ, who has blessed us with every spiritual blessing in the heavenly places in Christ,

DISCUSS

• Look at the passages one by one and discuss what you learned from marking each occurrence of *me, my, I, us, you.* As you do, discuss how each truth can help you handle fear or keep you from becoming fearful.

• Of all that you've seen, what one truth about God touches you the most?

4 just as He chose us in Him before the foundation of the world, that we would be holy and blameless before Him. In love

5 He predestined us to adoption as sons through Jesus Christ to Himself, according to the kind intention of His will.

EPHESIANS 2:8–10

8 For by grace you have been saved through faith; and that not of yourselves, it is the gift of God;

9 not as a result of works, so that no one may boast.

10 For we are His workmanship, created in Christ Jesus for good works, which God prepared beforehand so

that we would walk in them.

PSALM 138:8

The LORD will accomplish what concerns me;
Your lovingkindness,
O LORD, is everlasting;
do not forsake the works of Your hands.

1 JOHN 4:9–10, 18

9 By this the love of God was manifested in us, that God has sent His only begotten Son into the world so that we might live through Him.

10 In this is love, not that we loved God, but that He loved us and sent His Son to be the propitiation for our sins....

18 There is no fear in love; but perfect love

OBSERVE

Are you wondering, *What about God's love?* Good question! We saved this awesome insight for last.

Leader: Read 1 John 4:9–10, 18 aloud and have the group...

- *put a heart over every reference to **love**, like this:* ♡
- *draw a triangle over every reference to* ***God.***

Leader: Now read the passage again. This time have the group...

- *underline every **us, we, our, one.***
- *draw a jagged circle around each occurrence of **fear(s).***

DISCUSS

• What did you learn about God and love from these verses?

casts out fear, because fear involves punishment, and the one who fears is not perfected in love.

INSIGHT

The word *propitiation* means "satisfaction, payment." It speaks to the settling of a debt.

• What did you learn about you, if you are a true Christian—a person who has received and thus possesses Jesus Christ, the Son of God?

• What did you learn about fear?

• How does what you've seen in this passage shape your view of God? Your perspective on fear?

• Discuss any particular truths you learned in this lesson that will help you trust God more, so that you live in the fear of the Lord.

WRAP IT UP

You will find that the more you learn about God and His ways—especially from the Old Testament, because that is where God reveals His character and His power—the more you will be able to trust Him.

When the apostle Paul wrote his final letter telling Timothy of his impending death and urging him to guard the treasure of the Word of God, Paul began with this reminder: "For God gave us a spirit not of fear but of power and love and self-control" (2 Timothy 1:7, ESV).

Our study this week has certainly made you aware of the power of God, of His total sovereignty over good and over adversity. Now, couple that with the knowledge of the great love with which He loves you. You are chosen of God. Your life has purpose. You were created for good works—works that God Almighty chose for you.

Knowing this and the other truths you saw just in this one short lesson ought to greatly increase your reverence, your respect, your confidence, your trust in the Creator of the heavens and the earth, so that you say along with the prophet Jeremiah, "Nothing is too difficult for You" (32:17). To know this is to experience the fear of the Lord—a fear that can conquer every other fear. The fear of the Lord that gives you self-control in the face of fear.

In our next lesson we'll take a closer look at the fear of the Lord—the fear that frees you from all other fears. It will be a liberating study!

Wouldn't it be awesome to live free of fear? to be liberated from fears that assault your mind, trouble your soul, and bring untold anxiety, stress, and physical difficulties? to be unbothered by fear of man, of death, of life?

Perhaps you're thinking, *That's impossible!*

Well, according to God such freedom truly is possible—if you will learn to live in the fear of the Lord. The fear of the Lord brings all other fears into submission.

So what does the fear of the Lord look like—and how do we get it? That's where we'll start this week. We have an enlightening four weeks of study ahead of us on the fear of the Lord and how we can live day by day, moment by moment in its liberating power.

You might want to make Psalm 119:38 your prayer as you begin:

Establish Your word to Your servant, as that
which produces reverence for You.

OBSERVE

Let's look at some verses that define or describe the fear of the Lord. We will begin in Proverbs 1, which introduces the purpose of Proverbs and then defines the fear of the Lord.

PROVERBS 1:1–7

¹ The proverbs of Solomon the son of David, king of Israel:

² to know wisdom and instruction, to discern the sayings of understanding,

3 to receive instruction in wise behavior, righteousness, justice and equity;

4 to give prudence to the naive, to the youth knowledge and discretion,

5 a wise man will hear and increase in learning, and a man of understanding will acquire wise counsel,

6 to understand a proverb and a figure, the words of the wise and their riddles.

7 The fear of the LORD is the beginning of knowledge; fools despise wisdom and instruction.

Leader: *Read Proverbs 1:1–7; 8:12–14; and 9:10–11 aloud. Have the group say and…*

- *mark **wise** and **wisdom** with a* **W.**
- *double underline every occurrence of* **knowledge.**
- *draw a jagged circle around **the fear of the Lord:***

DISCUSS

- What did you learn about the purpose of the book of Proverbs?

  to Know wisdom

- Who is speaking in each of these verses?

  Solomon

- What did you learn about wisdom?

  increases

- What did you learn regarding knowledge?

  fear of the Lord.

- What did you learn about the fear of the Lord? *beginning of Knowledge*

INSIGHT

At least fifteen different Hebrew words are translated as *fear* in the Old Testament. It can refer to all sorts of fears common to man or to the fear of the Lord. The context in which each word is used determines how it is translated.

The fear of the Lord indicates respect, reverence, trust, obedience. It is the acknowledgment of what God says about Himself and His authority, which motivates us to respond accordingly and to seek knowledge and wisdom.

In the New Testament the basic Greek words translated as *fear* can also carry a range of meanings. As in the Old Testament, *the fear of the Lord* also carries the idea of respect and awe.

• What does Proverbs 1:7 tell you about the fear of the Lord?

Beginning of knowledge

PROVERBS 8:12–14

12 I, wisdom, dwell with prudence, and I find knowledge and discretion.

13 The fear of the LORD is to hate evil; pride and arrogance and the evil way and the perverted mouth, I hate.

14 Counsel is mine and sound wisdom; I am understanding, power is mine.

PROVERBS 9:10–11

10 The fear of the LORD is the beginning of wisdom, and the knowledge of the Holy One is understanding.

11 For by me your days will be multiplied, and years of life will be added to you.

• How important are knowledge and wisdom, and why?

INSIGHT

Proverbs tells us that the beginning, the starting point, of knowledge and wisdom is the fear of the Lord.

Knowledge "expresses a multitude of shades of knowledge gained by the senses."* Knowledge informs us, gives us insight that we can then act upon.

Wisdom describes our approach to life. There is a wisdom of man, of the world, and of God (1 Corinthians 1:19–21). The wisdom of God prompts us to approach life according to a correct knowledge of God. In 1 Corinthians 1:30 God tells us that Christ Jesus "became to us wisdom from God." Paul prayed that God would give the Ephesian believers "a spirit of wisdom and of revelation in the knowledge of Him" (Ephesians 1:17).

---

* R. Laird Harris, Gleason L. Archer Jr., and Bruce K. Waltke, eds., *Theological Wordbook of the Old Testament*, 2 vols. (Chicago, Moody, 1980), 1:366

OBSERVE

Early in the book of Proverbs, Solomon describes what happens to those who don't desire the wisdom of God.

Leader: Read Proverbs 1:23–31 aloud and have the group say and...
- *underline every **you, your, they, their**.*
- *mark each **I** and **my**, which in this passage refer to **wisdom**, with a **W**.*
- *draw a jagged circle around **the fear of the Lord**.*

DISCUSS

- What did you learn from marking *you, your, they,* and *their*? *foolish people.*

- How does all this relate to the fear of the Lord? How does it help you define the fear of the Lord? *Wisdom*

23 Turn to my reproof, behold, I will pour out my spirit on you; I will make my words known to you.

24 Because I called and you refused, I stretched out my hand and no one paid attention;

25 And you neglected all my counsel and did not want my reproof;

26 I will also laugh at your calamity; I will mock when your dread *fear* comes,

27 When your dread *fear* comes like a storm and your calamity comes like a whirlwind, when distress and anguish come upon you.

28 Then they will call on me, but I will not answer; they will seek me diligently but they will not find me,

29 because they hated knowledge and did not choose the fear of the LORD.

30 They would not accept my counsel, they spurned all my reproof.

31 So they shall eat of the fruit of their own way and be satiated with their own devices.

• When you think about what these verses tell us, how does it impact you? What feelings does it evoke? What actions or caution might result from these truths?

• Was there a time when this described you or someone you know? If so, what were the consequences?

OBSERVE

What about those who don't spurn wisdom? Let's continue reading Solomon's words to his son.

Leader: *Read Proverbs 2:1–12 aloud. Have the group...*
- *circle every reference to* **Solomon's son.**
- *mark each reference to* **wisdom,** *including the pronoun* **her,** *with a* **W.**
- *double underline every occurrence of* **knowledge.**
- *draw a jagged circle around* **the fear of the Lord.**

DISCUSS

- How does a person discern the fear of the Lord? *By Knowing G.W.*

PROVERBS 2:1–12

1 My son, if you will receive my words and treasure my commandments within you,

2 make your ear attentive to wisdom, incline your heart to understanding;

3 for if you cry for discernment, lift your voice for understanding;

4 if you seek her as silver and search for her as for hidden treasures;

5 then you will discern the fear of the LORD and discover the knowledge of God.

6 For the LORD gives wisdom; from His mouth come knowledge and understanding.

7 He stores up sound wisdom for the upright; He is a shield to those who walk in integrity,

8 guarding the paths of justice, and He preserves the way of His godly ones.

9 Then you will discern righteousness and justice and equity and every good course.

10 For wisdom will enter your heart and knowledge will be pleasant to your soul;

11 discretion will guard you, understanding will watch over you,

12 to deliver you from the way of evil, from the man who speaks perverse things.

- What did you learn from this passage about the source of wisdom and knowledge? How does this relate to the fear of the Lord? = G.W =

- What are the benefits gained from fear of the Lord, as described in verses 9–12?

  discernment
  wisdom satisfies
  deliver you –

- If you have children or grandchildren, how would you advise them in the light of what you have learned from Proverbs 1 and 2?

OBSERVE

Leader: *Read Proverbs 14:26–27 aloud.*

- *Have the group draw a jagged circle around **the fear of the Lord.***

DISCUSS

- What did you learn from marking *the fear of the Lord*?

- How does this compare with what you've already learned about the fear of the Lord?

PROVERBS 14:26–27

26 In the fear of the LORD there is strong confidence, and his children will have refuge.

not in yourself

27 The fear of the LORD is a fountain of life, that one may avoid the snares of death.

DEUTERONOMY 17:14, 18–20

14 When you enter the land which the LORD your God gives you, and you possess it and live in it, and you say, "I will set a king over me like all the nations who are around me."...

18 Now it shall come about when he sits on the throne of his kingdom, he shall write for himself a copy of this law on a scroll in the presence of the Levitical priests.

19 It shall be with him and he shall read it all the days of his life, that he may learn to fear the LORD his God, by carefully observing all the words of this law and these statutes,

OBSERVE

How does a person—whether royalty, a ruler, or a common ordinary citizen—acquire the fear of the Lord?

Leader: Read Deuteronomy 17:14, 18–20 and 31:10–12. Have the group…
- *draw a box around every reference to* **the law,** *including the pronoun* **it** *and the synonym* **commandment,** *like this:* ☐
- *draw a jagged circle around every reference to* **fearing the Lord.**
  W.O.G.

DISCUSS

- What did you learn from marking the references to the law, the commandments of the Lord?

- What did you learn from marking references to fearing the Lord God?

• According to what you have observed, how does one learn the fear of the Lord?

• In the first passage from Deuteronomy, who was instructed to fear the Lord God? How would this be accomplished and what was the purpose?

• What does this tell you about the value of fearing the Lord?

• In the second Deuteronomy passage, who is to fear the Lord and how would this happen?

• So if you desired the fear of the Lord, how would you get it? And what would it look like?

20 that his heart may not be lifted up above his countrymen and that he may not turn aside from the commandment, to the right or the left, so that he and his sons may continue long in his kingdom in the midst of Israel.

DEUTERONOMY 31:10–12

10 Then Moses commanded them, saying, "At the end of every seven years, at the time of the year of remission of debts, at the Feast of Booths,

11 when all Israel comes to appear before the LORD your God at the place which He will choose, you shall read this law in front of all Israel in their hearing.

12 "Assemble the people, the men and the women and children and the alien who is in your town, so that they may hear and learn and fear the LORD your God, and be careful to observe all the words of this law."

• From all you've learned, how do you think the fear of the Lord would help you deal with the fears of life?

• Are you willing to do what it takes to live in the fear of the Lord?

• What adjustments would you have to make?

• Are they worth it?

WRAP IT UP

As you look at your society, the culture in which you live, perhaps you see many who have simply destroyed their lives and you wonder why. What was missing in their lives that they pursued money, power, fame, sex, drugs, alcohol, their own immediate gratification at the expense of others or in exchange for their own future?

Would they have done so if they had walked in the fear of the Lord and pursued knowledge and wisdom? If they lived according to the wisdom and knowledge of God rather than according to the wisdom of man and his priorities, or the wisdom of this world that scorns the fear of the Lord and denies His authority in our lives?

In the United States of America, celebrity in its varied forms often becomes the standard by which people decide how to dress, walk, talk, behave, and set their priorities. The media ask celebrities to weigh in on issues of culture, politics, lifestyle. And the world listens to and follows them rather than God. The Bible is laid aside as archaic and irrelevant.

When one studies a true history of the United States of America, it is clear that this nation once boldly placed its trust in God. This declaration was printed on American money, carved on national monuments, written into the U.S. Constitution. In fact many of America's laws were based on God's laws, His commandments. To a certain degree, the fear of the Lord permeated the culture.

Now, the fear of the Lord is opposed, mocked, and often silenced by the intimidation of man. The values on which America was founded have been overruled by the will and whims of a society often opposed to the Word of God. Those who don't believe in the God of the Bible want to obliterate even the mention of His name and the precepts of His Word from public life.

You got a glimpse of what God says about Himself in the second lesson in this study. What will the Sovereign God do in and to America if this continues? The answer could impact the world.

So what is your role in light of all this? As you finish each lesson, review what you've learned. Think about it. You are studying the Word of God—truth. According to Jesus Christ, it is truth which keeps you from the evil one, that sets you apart, that teaches you the fear of the Lord (John 8:42–47; 17:14–17).

So learn the fear of the Lord, live in the fear of the Lord, teach the fear of the Lord to others. If they listen, continue. If they don't, shake the dust off your feet and search out others who will. You'll never know who will receive the message until you do what you are supposed to do. Listen to Jesus:

> *I have given them Your word; and the world has hated them,*
> *because they are not of the world, even as I am not of the*
> *world. I do not ask You to take them out of the world, but to*
> *keep them from the evil one. They are not of the world, even*
> *as I am not of the world. Sanctify them in the truth;*
> *Your word is truth. As You sent Me into the world, I also*
> *have sent them into the world. (John 17:14–18)*

Some things in life are worth living for—and worth dying for! Yet sometimes the fear of man, the fear of death, even fears about the daily challenges of life override our conviction and our passion for justice and truth.

We've seen how the fear of the Lord can prevail over all other fears, how a proper understanding of God's authority and our relationship with Him puts everything else into perspective. In the next few lessons, we'll consider further the truths we need to know and the things we need to do so that we will not be held captive by lesser fears—starting with the fear of man.

When we are threatened by man, whom we can see, hear, and feel, how can we press forward in confidence, believing in the God we can't see? We'll find the answer by looking at individuals in the Bible who learned how fear of the Lord could sustain them even in desperate situations. Let's see what God says and what they did.

OBSERVE

We'll begin by returning to a verse from an earlier lesson, a verse that highlights what God wants us to know about the fear of man and what it brings to our lives.

PROVERBS 29:25

The fear of man brings a snare, but he who trusts in the LORD will be exalted.

Leader: Read Proverbs 29:25 aloud with the group. Have them…
- *draw a jagged circle around **fear**.*
- *mark **trusts** with a big **T**.*

DISCUSS

• What two things are contrasted in this verse?

• What is the end result of fearing man?

• Based on what you've observed in your own life or in those around you, what are some of the traps, the snares, the actions that the fear of man can bring?

• As we saw in an earlier lesson, the word *exalted* means "secure, safe." So how can we achieve this status, according to this proverb?

OBSERVE

As we just saw, we can fear man or trust in God. The contrast is great once you know what man is like apart from God. Let's take a few minutes and get God's insight on mortal man.

Leader: Read Psalm 14:1–5 and Romans 3:10–18 aloud. Have the group…
- *underline every reference to **man**, beginning with **the fool**.*
- *draw a jagged circle around each occurrence of **dread** or **fear**.*

PSALM 14:1–5

1 The fool has said in his heart, "There is no God." They are corrupt, they have committed abominable deeds; there is no one who does good.

2 The LORD has looked down from heaven upon the sons of men to see if there are any who understand, who seek after God.

3 They have all turned aside, together they have become corrupt; there is no one who does good, not even one.

4 Do all the workers of wickedness not know, who eat up my people as they eat bread, and do not call upon the Lord?

5 There they are in great dread, for God is with the righteous generation.

ROMANS 3:10–18

10 There is none righteous, not even one;

11 there is none who understands, there is none who seeks for God;

12 all have turned aside, together they have become useless; there is none who does good, there is not even one.

13 Their throat is an open grave, with their tongues they keep deceiving. The poison of asps is under their lips;

14 whose mouth is full of cursing and bitterness;

DISCUSS

• What did you learn about people who do not fear God, love Him?

• When you encounter people like this or come under their authority or influence in any way, do you experience fear? If so, how do you deal with it?

15 their feet are swift to shed blood,

16 destruction and misery are in their paths,

17 and the path of peace they have not known.

18 There is no fear of God before their eyes.

OBSERVE

If these people don't belong to God, then who do they belong to?

Leader: Read aloud John 8:42–44; Ephesians 2:1–3; and Colossians 1:12–14. Have the group...

• *put a triangle over every reference to* **God,** *like this:* △

• *underline every* **you, we, them, us.**

• *mark every reference to* **the devil,** *including synonyms such as* **father, prince, spirit** *with a pitchfork like this:* ⚓

John 8:42–44

Jesus is speaking to religious leaders who do not believe in Him and would like to kill Him.

42 Jesus said to them, "If God were your Father, you would love Me, for I proceeded forth and have come from God, for I have not even come on My own initiative, but He sent Me.

43 "Why do you not understand what I am saying? It is because you cannot hear My word.

44 "You are of your father the devil, and you want to do the desires of your father. He was a murderer from the beginning, and does not stand in the truth because there is no truth in him. Whenever he speaks a lie, he speaks from his own nature, for he is a liar and the father of lies."

EPHESIANS 2:1–3

This was written to people who have been saved by the grace (the unearned favor) of God. Paul is explaining to them what they were like before they believed.

DISCUSS

• What did you learn in John 8 about those who don't believe in Jesus?

• Who is their father, and what is he like?

• What did you learn from the verses in Ephesians and Colossians about people before they become true Christians?

• What did you learn about God from these verses?

1 And you were dead in your trespasses and sins,

2 in which you formerly walked according to the course of this world, according to the prince of the power of the air, of the spirit that is now working in the sons of disobedience.

3 Among them we too all formerly lived in the lusts of our flesh, indulging the desires of the flesh and of the mind, and were by nature children of wrath, even as the rest.

• What did you learn from marking the references to the devil, the prince, the spirit? What is his kingdom, or domain?

COLOSSIANS 1:12–14

12 …giving thanks to the Father, who has qualified us to share in the inheritance of the saints in Light.

13 For He rescued us from the domain of darkness, and transferred us to the kingdom of His beloved Son,

14 in whom we have redemption, the forgiveness of sins.

PSALM 118:4–9

4 Oh let those who fear the LORD say, "His lovingkindness is everlasting."

5 From my distress I called upon the LORD; the LORD answered me and set me in a large place.

6 The LORD is for me; I will not fear; what can man do to me?

• How do these truths about ungodly people help explain why you should not allow the fear of man to rule you?

OBSERVE

So how does a person deal with the very real fear of man?

Leader: Read Psalm 118:4–9. Have the group...

- *draw a jagged circle around each occurrence of **fear**.*
- *underline every **my**, **I**, **me**.*
- *mark every reference to **trust** and **refuge** with a **T**.*

DISCUSS

- What did you learn from marking *my, I,* and *me*? Don't miss a thing about the relationship with the Lord described in these verses.

- What did you learn from marking *fear, trust,* and *refuge*?

- What did this person do when in distress, and how can you apply this to your life?

- The word *princes* in verse 9 refers to rulers. Do you think people trust more in their leaders than in God? Do they fear—or even respect—rulers more than God? Why?

- What have you learned about God in previous lessons that shapes your view about trusting our leaders to protect and rescue us rather than trusting God?

- How can knowing these truths help you practically?

7 The LORD is for me among those who help me; therefore I will look with satisfaction on those who hate me.

8 It is better to take refuge in the LORD than to trust in man.

9 It is better to take refuge in the LORD than to trust in princes.

DEUTERONOMY 20:1–4

1 When you go out to battle against your enemies and see horses and chariots and people more numerous than you, do not be afraid of them; for the LORD your God, who brought you up from the land of Egypt, is with you.

2 When you are approaching the battle, the priest shall come near and speak to the people.

3 He shall say to them, "Hear, O Israel, you are approaching the battle against your enemies today. Do not be fainthearted. Do not be afraid, or panic, or tremble before them,

OBSERVE

Let's do a little more digging and see what we can learn about how to deal with fear when we do battle with people who are enemies of God.

Leader: *Read Deuteronomy 20:1–4 and Psalm 115:9–11 aloud. Have the group do the following:*

- *Underline the references to **the people** —every **you, them.***
- *Draw a triangle over the references to **the Lord,** including pronouns.*
- *Draw a jagged circle around **afraid** and **fear.***
- *Mark **trust** with a* **T.**

DISCUSS

- Discuss Deuteronomy 20 first. What sort of situation was God preparing His people for?

- What were His instructions to the people?

- What did you learn from marking the references to the Lord? How would believing God, trusting what He said, help them not be frightened?

- What was their alternative to trusting God?

- Now look at Psalm 115:9–11 and discuss what you learned from marking the references to the Lord.

- What phrase is repeated in this passage? Why do you think it appears so many times?

- If you truly fear the Lord, what are you to do and why?

- Can God be trusted? How do you know?

⁴ for the LORD your God is the one who goes with you, to fight for you against your enemies, to save you."

PSALM 115:9–11

⁹ O Israel, trust in the LORD; He is their help and their shield.

¹⁰ O house of Aaron, trust in the LORD; He is their help and their shield.

¹¹ You who fear the LORD, trust in the LORD; He is their help and their shield.

2 CHRONICLES 20:1–12

¹ Now it came about after this that the sons of Moab and the sons of Ammon, together with some of the Meunites, came to make war against Jehoshaphat.

² Then some came and reported to Jehoshaphat, saying, "A great multitude is coming against you from beyond the sea, out of Aram and behold, they are in Hazazon-tamar (that is Engedi)."

³ Jehoshaphat was afraid and turned his attention to seek the LORD, and proclaimed a fast throughout all Judah.

⁴ So Judah gathered together to seek help

OBSERVE

Let's look at how one king responded to the threats of man. You'll find some great applications for your own life.

Leader: Read 2 Chronicles 20:1–12 and have the group...

- *underline the references to **Jehoshaphat**, including pronouns.*
- *draw a triangle over the references to **the Lord**, including pronouns.*
- *draw a jagged circle around **afraid**.*

DISCUSS

- What was Jehoshaphat's situation?

• According to verse 3, how did he feel about this? Is that a normal response?

from the LORD; they even came from all the cities of Judah to seek the LORD.

5 Then Jehoshaphat stood in the assembly of Judah and Jerusalem, in the house of the LORD before the new court,

• How would you feel if it were you?

6 and he said, "O LORD, the God of our fathers, are You not God in the heavens? And are You not ruler over all the kingdoms of the nations? Power and might are in Your hand so that no one can stand against You.

• What did Jehoshaphat do?

7 "Did You not, O our God, drive out the inhabitants of this land before Your people Israel and give it to the descendants of

Abraham Your friend forever?

8 "They have lived in it, and have built You a sanctuary there for Your name, saying,

9 'Should evil come upon us, the sword, or judgment, or pestilence, or famine, we will stand before this house and before You (for Your name is in this house) and cry to You in our distress, and You will hear and deliver us.'

10 "Now behold, the sons of Ammon and Moab and Mount Seir, whom You did not let Israel invade when they came out of the land of Egypt (they turned aside from

• What did you learn from marking the references to the Lord?

• How would knowing these things about the Lord help you or any other true child of God?

• What specific actions did Jehoshaphat take when he was afraid?

• What did you learn from this incident that you can apply when you are afraid of someone?

them and did not destroy them),

11 see how they are rewarding us by coming to drive us out from Your possession which You have given us as an inheritance.

12 "O our God, will You not judge them? For we are powerless before this great multitude who are coming against us; nor do we know what to do, but our eyes are on You."

2 CHRONICLES 20:14–15, 17, 20

14 Then in the midst of the assembly the Spirit of the LORD came upon Jahaziel...

15 and he said, "Listen, all Judah and the inhabitants of Jerusalem and King Jehoshaphat: thus says the LORD to you, 'Do not fear or be dismayed because of this great multitude, for the battle is not yours but God's....

17 "You need not fight in this battle; station yourselves, stand and see the salvation of the LORD on your behalf, O Judah and Jerusalem.' Do not fear or be dismayed; tomorrow go out to

OBSERVE

The story is not over. Let's see what happened next.

Leader: Read 2 Chronicles 20:14–15, 17, and 20. Have the group do the following:

- *Draw a triangle over every reference to* **the Lord, God.**
- *Underline the references to* **Jehoshaphat,** *including pronouns.*
- *Draw a jagged circle around the phrase* **do not fear or be dismayed.**
- *Mark* **trust** *with a* **T.**

DISCUSS

- What did you learn from marking the references to the Lord, God?

- What did Jehoshaphat urge the people to do in verse 20?

• How does this go with what you saw in Deuteronomy? (By the way, Moses was considered a prophet as well as the leader of Israel.)

• So who are they to put their trust in, who are they to fear—man who they can see or God whom they cannot see?

• There's not enough time to study what happened, but you know, don't you, who won? What lessons can you learn for your life when you are tempted to fear man rather than God?

face them, for the LORD is with you."…

20 They rose early in the morning and went out to the wilderness of Tekoa; and when they went out, Jehoshaphat stood and said, "Listen to me, O Judah and inhabitants of Jerusalem, put your trust in the LORD your God and you will be established. Put your trust in His prophets and succeed."

JOSHUA 1:1–3, 7–9

¹ Now it came about after the death of Moses the servant of the LORD, that the LORD spoke to Joshua the son of Nun, Moses' servant, saying,

² "Moses My servant is dead; now therefore arise, cross this Jordan, you and all this people, to the land which I am giving to them, to the sons of Israel.

³ "Every place on which the sole of your foot treads, I have given it to you, just as I spoke to Moses....

⁷ "Only be strong and very courageous; be careful to do according to all the law which Moses My

OBSERVE

Let's see how we can make sure we walk in the fear of the Lord rather than in fear of man.

Leader: Read Joshua 1:1–3, 7–9 and have the group...

- *mark each reference to **Joshua,** including pronouns, with a **J.***
- *draw a jagged circle around any word or phrase that would indicate **fear.***
- *draw a box around the references to **the law** and **the book of the law.***
- *draw a cloud shape like this* {☁} *around **strong and courageous.***

DISCUSS

- Look at the places where you marked *Joshua.* What were God's instructions to him?

- What did God tell Joshua that gave him confidence?

INSIGHT

The definitions of the Hebrew words used in Joshua 1 give us a clear and memorable word picture of what God was saying:

Strong means "to fasten on to, to seize or grip."

Courageous means "to be alert, physically and mentally. To not fall apart."

Dismayed means "to break down by violence, confusion, fear."

To fail is "to slacken, to let drop, abandon."

To forsake is similar to fail, as it means "to loosen, relinquish, depart, abandon."

The book of the law is the Torah, the first five books of the Bible: Genesis, Exodus, Leviticus, Numbers, and Deuteronomy. Every king was to write his own copy of the law.

• What did you learn from marking the references to the law, the book of the law?

servant commanded you; do not turn from it to the right or to the left, so that you may have success wherever you go.

8 "This book of the law shall not depart from your mouth, but you shall meditate on it day and night, so that you may be careful to do according to all that is written in it; for then you will make your way prosperous, and then you will have success.

9 "Have I not commanded you? Be strong and courageous! Do not tremble or be dismayed, for the LORD your God is with you wherever you go."

- Did God suggest to Joshua that giving attention to the book of the law was optional?

- In light of this, how important do you think the Word of God is when it comes to the fear of man and the fear of God?

- What did you learn from 2 Chronicles 20 about Jehoshaphat's knowledge of God and God's promises and instructions to His people? (Just think, Joshua and Jehoshaphat only had five books of the Bible; you have all sixty-six!)

- What has been your attitude toward the Word of God and how has it shaped your actions, your approach to life's circumstances?

- What place does the Word of God hold in your daily life? How does that compare with God's instruction to Joshua in verse 8?

• Describe a time when your knowledge of the Word of God helped you avoid the snare of the fear of man. If you cannot think of one, what does that suggest to you?

OBSERVE

Let's close this week's study by turning to three passages in the New Testament that might help bring Joshua 1:7–9 home to your heart.

Leader: *Read aloud John 16:33; Hebrews 13:5–6; and Ephesians 6:10–11. Have the group do the following:*

- *Put a cross over every reference to **Jesus.***
- *Put a triangle over every reference to **the Lord, God.***
- *Underline every reference to **the disciples** or **the recipients of the message.***
- *Draw a jagged circle around any reference to **being afraid.***
- *Draw a cloud around any reference to **courage, strength,** or **being strong.***

JOHN 16:33

These things I [*Jesus*] have spoken to you [*the disciples*], so that in Me you may have peace. In the world you have tribulation, but take courage; I have overcome the world.

HEBREWS 13:5–6

5 Make sure that your character is free from the love of money, being content with what you have; for He Himself has said, "I will never desert you, nor will I ever forsake you,"

⁶ so that we confidently say, "The Lord is my helper, I will not be afraid. What will man do to me?"

EPHESIANS 6:10–11

¹⁰ Finally, be strong in the Lord and in the strength of His might.

¹¹ Put on the full armor of God, so that you will be able to stand firm against the schemes of the devil.

DISCUSS

• What did you learn from marking the references to the Lord?

• What did you learn from marking *afraid, strong,* and *courage*?

• Review what you learned from the Insight box, which is reprinted on the next page for your convenience. Discuss how understanding those words, and knowing the verses from Joshua and the New Testament, can help you walk in the fear of the Lord rather than the fear of man.

INSIGHT

The definitions of the Hebrew words used in Joshua 1 give us a clear and memorable word picture of what God was saying:

Strong means "to fasten on to, to seize or grip."

Courageous means "to be alert, physically and mentally. To not fall apart."

Dismayed means "to break down by violence, confusion, fear."

To fail is "to slacken, to let drop, abandon."

To forsake is similar to fail, as it means "to loosen, relinquish, depart, abandon."

• Finally, how could the love of money keep you—or others—from the fear of God? Do you think this is an issue today? Discuss that with the group.

WRAP IT UP

Throughout our lives each of us will confront and have to deal with the fear of man. The only fear that can override the fear of man in its many forms is the fear of the Lord, which means we need to continually strengthen and renew our understanding of Him.

Here are three suggestions on how to do that.

First, get in the Word of God daily—not out of mere duty but because we live by every word that comes from His mouth (Deuteronomy 8:3; Matthew 4:4). Learn to study God's Word "inductively"— firsthand so that God Himself teaches you, as Psalm 119:102 says. Precept Ministries International's mission is to establish people in God's Word so that it produces reverence for God—the fear of the Lord. The ministry has all the tools to teach and train you how to discover truth for yourself, go deeper with others, and disciple—online or in print. PMI is in more than 150 countries and 70 languages and has materials for children, teens, and adults. The book you are using was produced by this ministry.*

Second, the more you actually choose the fear of the Lord—trusting in Him and doing what He says no matter the circumstances—the stronger you will become spiritually. Walking in the fear of the Lord will bring such a deep sense of peace and the favor of God that you'll long for it more and more.

Third, stay in fellowship with other strong believers who will be there to support you and, if necessary, to correct you. God puts us in a

---

* For more information on our resources, visit www.precept.org.

body because we need each other. "A cord of three strands is not quickly torn apart" (Ecclesiastes 4:12).

Next week we'll consider the fear of death—a reality we all need to know how to confront with strength and courage.

And you are not to fear what they fear or be in dread of it.
It is the LORD of hosts whom you should regard as holy.
And He shall be your fear, and He shall be your dread.
Then He shall become a sanctuary. (Isaiah 8:12–14)

The fear of death is a powerful motivator. If those who rule by might and intimidation cannot subdue an individual to their will, then they use the threat of death. It's the ultimate weapon, powered by a fear so strong that it can crumple a person to his knees, cause him to deny his beliefs, compel him to betray others.

But not everyone is vulnerable to this threat. The convinced and courageous prefer to die for what they believe. The records of history tell us that the blood of the martyrs was the seed of the church. Instead of eradicating the faithful, persecution and martyrdom marked the rapid growth of the early church.

What did the Christians believe that enabled them to die so valiantly? What gave them the strength and courage to die in faith rather than deny Jesus Christ and His precepts of life?

In this lesson we'll see how the fear of the Lord—understanding His dominion over life and the grave—can conquer the fear of death.

OBSERVE

In Genesis, the book of beginnings, we find the very first reference to death and to being afraid. When God created Adam and Eve, He put them in a perfect environment and gave them only one restriction: do not eat of the fruit of the tree of the knowledge of good and evil. God made clear what would happen if they disobeyed. But enticed by the serpent, the devil, Eve ate

GENESIS 2:16–17; 3:7–10

16 The LORD God commanded the man, saying, "From any tree of the garden you may eat freely;

17 but from the tree of the knowledge of good and evil you shall

not eat, for in the day that you eat from it you will surely die."…

3:7 Then the eyes of both of them were opened, and they knew that they were naked; and they sewed fig leaves together and made themselves loin coverings.

8 They heard the sound of the LORD God walking in the garden in the cool of the day, and the man and his wife hid themselves from the presence of the LORD God among the trees of the garden.

9 Then the LORD God called to the man, and said to him, "Where are you?"

the forbidden fruit. She gave it to Adam and he ate also.

Leader: Read Genesis 2:16–17 and 3:7–10. Have the group say and…
- *draw a triangle over every reference to* **the Lord God.**
- *mark the word* **die** *with a tombstone, like this:* ⌂
- *draw a jagged circle around* **afraid.**

DISCUSS

- What did you learn from marking *die*— the very first reference to death in the Word of God?

- To be sure you don't miss it, what action would result in death? Can you summarize it in one word?

• What did Adam and Eve do in respect to God when they disobeyed?

OBSERVE

Sin brings death, which separates us from God, who is life.

Leader: Read Romans 5:12 and 6:23. Have the group…
  • *mark* **sin** *with a big* **S.**
  • *mark each occurrence of the word* **death** *with a tombstone.*
  • *draw a triangle over* **God.**

DISCUSS

• What did you learn from marking *death*?

• What did you learn from marking *God*?

10 He said, "I heard the sound of You in the garden, and I was afraid because I was naked; so I hid myself."

ROMANS 5:12

Therefore, just as through one man sin entered into the world, and death through sin, and so death spread to all men, because all sinned.

ROMANS 6:23

For the wages of sin is death, but the free gift of God is eternal life in Christ Jesus our Lord.

HEBREWS 2:9, 14–15

9 But we do see Him who was made for a little while lower than the angels, namely, Jesus, because of the suffering of death crowned with glory and honor, so that by the grace of God He might taste death for everyone....

14 Therefore, since the children share in flesh and blood, He Himself likewise also partook of the same, that through death He might render powerless him who had the power of death, that is, the devil,

15 and might free those who through fear of death were subject to slavery all their lives.

OBSERVE

So how does eternal life come through Jesus Christ? How does God give life to people who are born sinners and are therefore destined for death, eternal separation from God, who is life?

Leader: Read aloud Hebrews 2:9, 14–15 and 2 Corinthians 5:21. Have the group...

- *mark every reference to **Jesus,** including pronouns, with a cross:* †
- *mark each occurrence of the word **death** with a tombstone.*
- *draw a jagged circle around **fear.***

DISCUSS

• What did you learn from marking *Jesus?* It's awesome, and it pertains to you, so don't miss a thing!

• Why does God stress that Jesus was made lower than the angels, that He became flesh and blood—a human being?

• Who was it who sinned in Genesis 3, and what result did that sin bring? What did you see in Romans 5:12? Review it.

• So what did you learn from marking *death* in Hebrews?

• According to Romans 6:23, which you just looked at, what brings death?

• So what gave the devil, the serpent, the power of death over man, as described in Hebrews 2:14?

• And how was man's sin taken care of, paid for?

• So, if you are a true believer in Jesus Christ, if you fear God and believe in Jesus Christ, what kind of life do you have? Will you ever be separated from God and Jesus Christ? Explain your answer.

> **2 CORINTHIANS 5:21**
>
> He [*God*] made Him [*Jesus*] who knew no sin to be sin on our behalf, so that we might become the righteousness of God in Him.

1 John 5:11–13

11 And the testimony is this, that God has given us eternal life, and this life is in His Son.

12 He who has the Son has the life; he who does not have the Son of God does not have the life.

13 These things I have written to you who believe in the name of the Son of God, so that you may know that you have eternal life.

OBSERVE

Leader: Read 1 John 5:11–13. Have the group...

- circle each occurrence of the phrase **eternal life** and the word **life.**
- mark every reference to **the Son of God** with a cross.
- draw a tombstone over the phrase **does not have the life.**

DISCUSS

- What has God given us and how do we get it?

- What is our situation if we don't have Jesus Christ, the Son of God?

OBSERVE

So what happens to a Christian when he or she dies physically? Let's see what the apostle Paul wrote under the inspiration of God.

Leader: *Read Philippians 1:21–23; 2 Corinthians 5:6–8; and Romans 8:38–39. Have the group…*

- *underline every pronoun that refers to **Paul** or to **fellow believers**, including **me**, **I**, **we**, **us**.*
- *draw a tombstone over each of these words or phrases: **die, depart, absent from the body, death.***

DISCUSS

- What did you learn from marking *me, I, we,* and *us?*

INSIGHT

Paul wrote his letter to the Philippians from prison in Rome. Eventually this man who lived in the fear of God was beheaded for his faith.

PHILIPPIANS 1:21–23

21 For to me, to live is Christ and to die is gain.

22 But if I am to live on in the flesh, this will mean fruitful labor for me; and I do not know which to choose.

23 But I am hard-pressed from both directions, having the desire to depart and be with Christ, for that is very much better.

2 CORINTHIANS 5:6–8

6 Therefore, being always of good courage, and knowing that while we are at home in the body we are absent from the Lord—

7 for we walk by faith, not by sight—

8 we are of good courage, I say, and prefer rather to be absent from the body and to be at home with the Lord.

ROMANS 8:38–39

38 For I am convinced that neither death, nor life, nor angels, nor principalities, nor things present, nor things to come, nor powers,

39 nor height, nor depth, nor any other created thing, will be able to separate us from the love of God, which is in Christ Jesus our Lord.

• What did you learn from marking the references to dying, departing, being absent from the body, and death?

• Did you already know this? How does this truth affect your perspective on death for the Christian?

• The fear of the Lord is demonstrated by acknowledging truth and living accordingly. How would this truth affect the way you live and die? And how does this go with courage as seen in 2 Corinthians 5:7–8?

OBSERVE

If you fear the Lord, does that mean you won't die at the hands of others?

Leader: Read Luke 12:4–7 and Matthew 10:26–28 aloud—slowly. Note that Jesus is speaking in both passages. Have the group...
- *draw a jagged circle around every occurrence of the words **afraid** and **fear.***
- *draw a tombstone over the words **kill(ed)** and **destroy.***

DISCUSS

- What did you learn from marking *afraid* and *fear?*

- Who are you to fear, and why?

LUKE 12:4–7

4 I say to you, My friends, do not be afraid of those who kill the body and after that have no more that they can do.

5 But I will warn you whom to fear: fear the One who, after He has killed, has authority to cast into hell; yes, I tell you, fear Him!

6 Are not five sparrows sold for two cents? Yet not one of them is forgotten before God.

7 Indeed, the very hairs of your head are all numbered. Do not fear; you are more valuable than many sparrows.

Matthew 10:26–28

26 Therefore do not fear them, for there is nothing concealed that will not be revealed, or hidden that will not be known.

27 What I tell you in the darkness, speak in the light; and what you hear whispered in your ear, proclaim upon the housetops.

28 Do not fear those who kill the body but are unable to kill the soul; but rather fear Him who is able to destroy both soul and body in hell.

• What does such knowledge mean to you? How could it affect your life, your ministry, your message—your witness to others—if you truly believed it and lived accordingly?

• Have you ever known or read of someone who died for their faith? How did it affect you?

OBSERVE

So who determines when we die—or is that up to chance?

Leader: *Read Psalm 139:16 and Deuteronomy 32:39. Have the group…*
- *put a triangle over every reference to* ***God.*** *Watch carefully for the pronouns.*
- *draw a tombstone over* ***death.***

DISCUSS

- What did you learn from marking the references to God?

- What did you learn about who determines your death and when it comes?

- How would believing what you just read help you deal with the fear of death?

- Do you believe it? If you don't, are you fearing the Lord? And what would be the end result of not believing? Explain your answer.

PSALM 139:16

The psalmist is speaking of God.

Your eyes have seen my unformed substance; and in Your book were all written the days that were ordained for me, when as yet there was not one of them.

DEUTERONOMY 32:39

God is speaking.

See now that I, I am He, and there is no god besides Me; it is I who put to death and give life. I have wounded and it is I who heal, and there is no one who can deliver from My hand.

REVELATION 2:8–11

8 And to the angel of the church in Smyrna write: The first and the last, who was dead, and has come to life, says this:

9 "I know your tribulation and your poverty (but you are rich), and the blasphemy by those who say they are Jews and are not, but are a synagogue of Satan.

10 "Do not fear what you are about to suffer. Behold, the devil is about to cast some of you into prison, so that you will be tested, and you will have tribulation for ten days. Be faithful until death, and I will give you the crown of life.

OBSERVE

The second and third chapters of Revelation comprise seven letters of Jesus to seven churches in Asia. Each letter ends with a promise to overcomers.

Leader: Read Revelation 2:8–11 and have the group do the following:
- *Mark the references to **Jesus, the first and the last,** with a cross.*
- *Underline every pronoun referring to **believers: your, you, he, him.***
- *Draw a jagged circle around the phrase **do not fear.***
- *Draw a tombstone over the words **dead** and **death.***

INSIGHT

According to 1 John 5:4–5, the one who overcomes is a person who is born of God—one who believes that Jesus is the Son of God. Their faith is the victory that overcomes the world.

DISCUSS

• What kind of message did Jesus give to the church of Smyrna? Would you describe it as hard? Easy? Shocking? Scary? Why?

• What did you learn from marking *you* and *your*? Be very thorough in your answers.

• How did Jesus Christ describe Himself in verse 8?

• Do you see any connection between this description and what He tells the church? Explain your answer.

• What did you learn from marking the references to death?

(If you're wondering what is meant by the second death, hang in with us just a little longer and we'll look together at the answer.)

11 "He who has an ear, let him hear what the Spirit says to the churches. He who overcomes will not be hurt by the second death."

REVELATION 1:12–13, 17–18

12 Then I turned to see the voice that was speaking with me. And having turned I saw seven golden lampstands; ...

13 and in the middle of the lampstands I saw one like a son of man, clothed in a robe reaching to the feet, and girded across His chest with a golden sash....

17 When I saw Him, I fell at His feet like a dead man. And He placed His right hand on me, saying, "Do not be afraid; I am the first and the last,

18 and the living One; and I was dead, and behold, I am alive

OBSERVE

Let's take another look at the One who spoke to the church at Smyrna. He appears in the apostle John's description of a vision he saw in the Spirit during his exile on the isle of Patmos, the persecution he suffered for his faithful witness to the Word of God and the testimony of Jesus Christ. John is the "I" of the passage we will observe.

Leader: Read Revelation 1:12–13, 17–18 and have the group...

- *put a cross over every reference to **the one like a son of man,** including pronouns.*
- *draw a jagged circle around the phrase **do not be afraid.***
- *mark the words **dead** and **death** with a tombstone.*

DISCUSS

- What did you learn from verses 17–18 about the One John saw?

- Who do you think this is, and why?

• Why are we not to be afraid? What did you learn, again, about death?

OBSERVE

Will there ever be an end to death? Let's read John's prophecy of what will happen following Jesus' thousand-year reign on the earth.

Leader: Read Revelation 20:11–21:8 slowly. Have the group…
> • *put a triangle over every reference to* **God, Him, He,** *and* **His.**
> • *mark the words* **dead** *and* **death** *with a tombstone.*

DISCUSS

• What did you learn from marking the references to God in Revelation 20:11–14? Include what you see about the throne of God in verse 12.

---

forevermore, and I have the keys of death and of Hades.

REVELATION 20:11–21:8

11 Then I saw a great white throne and Him who sat upon it, from whose presence earth and heaven fled away, and no place was found for them.

12 And I saw the dead, the great and the small, standing before the throne, and books were opened; and another book was opened, which is the book of life; and the dead were judged from the things which were written in the books, according to their deeds.

13 And the sea gave up the dead which were in it, and death

and Hades gave up the dead which were in them; and they were judged, every one of them according to their deeds.

14 Then death and Hades were thrown into the lake of fire. This is the second death, the lake of fire.

15 And if anyone's name was not found written in the book of life, he was thrown into the lake of fire.

21:1 Then I saw a new heaven and a new earth; for the first heaven and the first earth passed away, and there is no longer any sea.

2 And I saw the holy city, new Jerusalem, coming down out of

• What did you learn from marking the references to the dead and death in Revelation 20:11–15?

• Now, let's think for a minute. Will all those who tortured and put to death the children of God, such as those you read about in Smyrna, get away with it? How do you know?

• As you observed Revelation 21:1–8, what did you learn from marking the references to God?

• What did you learn about death from this passage?

• We saw in week 4 that God commanded Joshua to be strong and courageous—to meditate on God's Word, then to obey it. He wasn't to turn to the right or left, but was to be careful to do according to all God had commanded (Joshua 1:7). Surely that is the fear of the Lord in action. But what about those who don't? Look at Revelation 21:8. How are those who experience the second death described?

• Did they have an opportunity to escape? And why didn't they?

heaven from God, made ready as a bride adorned for her husband.

[3] And I heard a loud voice from the throne, saying, "Behold, the tabernacle of God is among men, and He will dwell among them, and they shall be His people, and God Himself will be among them,

[4] and He will wipe away every tear from their eyes; and there will no longer be any death; there will no longer be any mourning, or crying, or pain; the first things have passed away."

[5] And He who sits on the throne said, "Behold, I am making all things new." And He said,

"Write, for these words are faithful and true."

6 Then He said to me, "It is done. I am the Alpha and the Omega, the beginning and the end. I will give to the one who thirsts from the spring of the water of life without cost.

7 "He who overcomes will inherit these things, and I will be his God and he will be My son.

8 "But for the cowardly and unbelieving and abominable and murderers and immoral persons and sorcerers and idolaters and all liars, their part will be in the lake that burns with fire and brimstone, which is the second death."

• Is your name in the book of life? How do you know?

• If your name is not in the book of life, what do you need to do?

• If it is, do you need to fear death? Explain your answer.

• What fear have you chosen?

WRAP IT UP

Does it bring comfort and confidence to know these truths for yourself? That you cannot die without God's permission and that—no matter how you die—if you belong to Him, to be absent from the body is to be present with the Lord?

Does such knowledge help you live in the fear of the Lord, embracing His Word as truth, trusting Him, respecting Him, reverencing Him for who He is? To do so would be wisdom—and life.

Life can be so uncertain, and that uncertainty often leads to fear. We can find ourselves continually worried about the *what ifs* of life. *What will happen to me, to my loved one, if* _____ *?* If what? We could all fill in the blanks with our own "ifs," couldn't we?

But are we to live in fear of what our lives may bring between now and death? In anxiety about what the future holds? Are we to get caught up in the roller coaster of excitement and dread, with our emotions determined by what is happening around us, what we are experiencing, what we are told is coming?

As we began our study, we asked ourselves the question Jesus asked His disciples: "Why are you afraid?" Then we looked at who God is—truths about Him and His Son that bring confidence as we believe His promise, "I am with you." We explored a little of what it is to know and to trust the One who is present with us in every storm!

In the third week of our study we looked at the one fear that subdues and conquers all other fears: the fear of the Lord. In week four we looked at how to overcome the fear of man that threatens to hold us captive. Then last week we looked at how we can deal with the fear of death.

This week we want to see practically how a person can conquer the fear of uncertainty as well as anxiety about matters of daily life by living moment by moment in the fear of the Lord. May God use it in such a way that you find yourself living life on a higher plane, walking confidently with the Light of life (John 8:12).

ISAIAH 50:10, ESV

Who among you fears the LORD and obeys the voice of his servant? Let him who walks in darkness and has no light trust in the name of the LORD and rely on his God.

PSALM 27:1–3

¹ The LORD is my light and my salvation; whom shall I fear? The LORD is the defense of my life; whom shall I dread?

² When evildoers came upon me to devour my flesh, my adversaries and my enemies, they stumbled and fell.

³ Though a host encamp against me, my heart will not fear;

OBSERVE

God never intends for people to walk in darkness. Darkness is the womb from which fear is born.

Leader: Read Isaiah 50:10; Psalm 27:1–3; and John 8:12 aloud. Have the group...

- *underline every pronoun—__who, you, him, me, my, I,__ and __them__—when it refers to a person other than God or Jesus.*
- *draw a semicircle over every occurrence of the word __darkness,__ like this:*
- *draw a jagged circle around the phrase __fears the Lord__ and around the words __fear__ and __dread.__*

DISCUSS

- What did you learn from marking the pronouns such as *who, you,* and *him*? Note the various situations mentioned in these verses.

• How does a person escape darkness?

• What does this have to do with the fear of the Lord?

OBSERVE

God is to be served with "single-eyed" devotion—with all our trust placed solely in Him. Consider what Jesus taught on one of the small mountains near the shore of the Galilee.

Leader: *Read Matthew 6:22, 24–34 slowly. Have the group…*
  • *underline every **your**, **you**, **no one**, **he**, **we.***
  • *draw a jagged circle around every reference to **worry** or **being worried.***

though war arise against me, in spite of this I shall be confident.

JOHN 8:12

Then Jesus again spoke to them, saying, "I am the Light of the world; he who follows Me will not walk in the darkness, but will have the Light of life."

MATTHEW 6:22, 24–34

22 The eye is the lamp of the body; so then if your eye is clear, your whole body will be full of light.…

24 No one can serve two masters; for either he will hate the one and love the other, or he will be devoted to one and despise the other. You cannot serve God and wealth.

25 For this reason I say to you, do not be worried about your life, as to what you will eat or what you will drink; nor for your body, as to what you will put on. Is not life more than food, and the body more than clothing?

26 Look at the birds of the air, that they do not sow, nor reap nor gather into barns, and yet your heavenly Father feeds them. Are you not worth much more than they?

27 And who of you by being worried can add a single hour to his life?

28 And why are you worried about cloth-ing? Observe how the

DISCUSS

• What did you learn from marking *you* and *your*?

• What did you learn from marking the references to worry?

• How do these references to worry relate to the fears we face in life? Share your insights with the group.

• So what answer did Jesus give to these worries of life?

lilies of the field grow; they do not toil nor do they spin,

29 yet I say to you that not even Solomon in all his glory clothed himself like one of these.

30 But if God so clothes the grass of the field, which is alive today and tomorrow is thrown into the furnace, will He not much more clothe you? You of little faith!

31 Do not worry then, saying, "What will we eat?" or "What will we drink?" or "What will we wear for clothing?"

32 For the Gentiles eagerly seek all these things; for your heavenly Father knows that you need all these things.

33 But seek first His kingdom and His righteousness, and all these things will be added to you.

34 So do not worry about tomorrow; for tomorrow will care for itself. Each day has enough trouble of its own.

Hebrews 4:14–16

14 Therefore, since we have a great high priest who has passed through the heavens, Jesus the Son of God, let us hold fast our confession.

15 For we do not have a high priest who cannot sympathize with our weaknesses, but One who has been tempted in all things

• If you seek God and His kingdom above all else, then are you living in the fear of the Lord? Explain your answer.

OBSERVE

Jesus taught His disciples to keep a single eye, to focus not on money but on God. He instructed us not to worry about even the most mundane needs of life, but to seek first God's kingdom. But does Jesus really understand the difficulties we face?

Leader: Read Hebrews 4:14–16 aloud and have the group…

• *underline every **we, us, our.***
• *put a cross over every reference to our **high priest, Jesus,** including pronouns and synonyms.*

DISCUSS

• What did you learn from marking the references to Jesus?

• What did you learn from marking *we, us,* and *our*?

• How can knowing this help you confront fear in difficult situations?

OBSERVE

In prophesying about the Messiah, Isaiah told us that the fear of the Lord would rest on Jesus, that He would delight in the fear of the Lord (Isaiah 11:1–3). So how did Jesus, God in the flesh of man, live while here on earth? And what are we to do with this knowledge?

Leader: *Read aloud John 5:30; 14:10; 1 Corinthians 11:1; 1 John 2:6.*

> • *Have the group put a cross over every reference to* **Jesus,** *including* **I, My, Me, Christ, Him, He.**

as we are, yet without sin.

16 Therefore let us draw near with confidence to the throne of grace, so that we may receive mercy and find grace to help in time of need.

John 5:30

Jesus is speaking.

I can do nothing on My own initiative. As I hear, I judge; and My judgment is just, because I do not seek My own will, but the will of Him who sent Me.

John 14:10

Jesus is speaking.

Do you not believe that I am in the

Father, and the Father is in Me? The words that I say to you I do not speak on My own initiative, but the Father abiding in Me does His works.

1 Corinthians 11:1

Paul is writing.

Be imitators of me, just as I also am of Christ.

1 John 2:6

The one who says he abides in Him [*Jesus*] ought himself to walk in the same manner as He walked.

DISCUSS

• What did you learn about the way Jesus conducted His life?

• If to fear the Lord means to trust in Him, to reverence Him, believing and obeying what He says, then how did Jesus demonstrate the fear of the Lord in His life?

• Why is knowing this important to you as a child of God? What lesson is in this for you? Explain your answer.

OBSERVE

As a child of God, how are you to live all the days of your life?

Leader: Read Jeremiah 17:5–8 and Proverbs 3:5–8 aloud. Have the group…
- *underline every reference to **the one being spoken about** or **the one being spoken to**. So you would underline **you, your, man, he**.*
- *draw a jagged circle around the words **fear** and **anxious**.*
- *mark each occurrence of **trust(s)** with a **T**.*

DISCUSS

- What contrasts and comparisons are used in Jeremiah 17:5–8?

- What did you learn about the person described in verses 5–6 of Jeremiah?

JEREMIAH 17:5–8

5 Thus says the LORD, "Cursed is the man who trusts in mankind and makes flesh his strength, and whose heart turns away from the LORD.

6 "For he will be like a bush in the desert and will not see when prosperity comes, but will live in stony wastes in the wilderness, a land of salt without inhabitant.

7 "Blessed is the man who trusts in the LORD and whose trust is the LORD.

8 "For he will be like a tree planted by the water, that extends its roots by a stream and will not fear when the

heat comes; but its leaves will be green, and it will not be anxious in a year of drought nor cease to yield fruit."

PROVERBS 3:5–8

5 Trust in the LORD with all your heart and do not lean on your own understanding.

6 In all your ways acknowledge Him, and He will make your paths straight.

7 Do not be wise in your own eyes; fear the LORD and turn away from evil.

8 It will be healing to your body and refreshment to your bones.

• What did you learn about the person in Jeremiah 17:7–8 and from the illustration of the tree? How does this apply to our lives?

• What are some ways "the heat comes" (Jeremiah 17:8) to our lives?

• Now, what did you learn from marking *your* in Proverbs 3?

• What does the fear of the Lord look like in these verses?

• What practical insights do these verses give you into the *how* of fearing the Lord?

• What benefits, if any, come through fearing the Lord?

OBSERVE

David, when caught by his enemy Abimelech, feigned madness and was released. Afterward he wrote Psalm 34. When you are confronted with the fears of life, you'll find his words can bring you such comfort. Let's look at it now and see what we can learn from his example.

Leader: Read Psalm 34:4–19 aloud—slowly. Have the group…

- *underline every reference to **the psalmist** and **the person who takes refuge in God**, such as **I**, **me**, **they**, **the righteous**.*
- *draw a jagged circle around any reference to **fear**.*

DISCUSS

Leader: Move through the psalm one segment at a time. You will notice some verse numbers are underlined. This is to help you divide the psalm into sections for discussion. For each segment discuss the following:

PSALM 34:4–19

4 I sought the LORD, and He answered me, and delivered me from all my fears.

5 They looked to Him and were radiant, and their faces will never be ashamed.

6 This poor man cried, and the LORD heard him and saved him out of all his troubles.

7 The angel of the LORD encamps around those who fear Him, and rescues them.

8 O taste and see that the LORD is good; how blessed is the man who takes refuge in Him!

9 O fear the LORD, you His saints; for to

those who fear Him there is no want.

10 The young lions do lack and suffer hunger; but they who seek the LORD shall not be in want of any good thing.

11 Come, you children, listen to me; I will teach you the fear of the LORD.

12 Who is the man who desires life and loves length of days that he may see good?

13 Keep your tongue from evil and your lips from speaking deceit.

14 Depart from evil and do good; seek peace and pursue it.

15 The eyes of the LORD are toward the

• What did you learn in these particular verses about those who seek the Lord, who cry to Him? What did they do or what are they instructed to do?

• How does God respond?

Leader: *After you've covered the preceding questions for all segments, discuss these additional questions about verse 19:*

• What did you observe in verse 19?

• What does this tell you about the fears of life? Is there any comfort here? Explain your answer.

righteous and His ears are open to their cry.

16 The face of the LORD is against evildoers, to cut off the memory of them from the earth.

17 The righteous cry, and the LORD hears and delivers them out of all their troubles.

18 The LORD is near to the brokenhearted and saves those who are crushed in spirit.

19 Many are the afflictions of the righteous, but the LORD delivers him out of them all.

ISAIAH 41:10

Do not fear, for I am with you; do not anxiously look about you, for I am your God. I will strengthen you, surely I will help you, surely I will uphold you with My righteous right hand.

MALACHI 3:16–4:3

16 Then those who feared the LORD spoke to one another, and the LORD gave attention and heard it, and a book of remembrance was written before Him for those who fear the LORD and who esteem His name.

17 "They will be Mine," says the LORD of hosts, "on the day

OBSERVE

But what is your responsibility? What are you to do when you encounter life's difficulties, tests, trials? And how will God respond?

Leader: Read Isaiah 41:10 and Malachi 3:16–4:3 aloud. Have the group...
- *draw a jagged circle over every occurrence of the words **fear(ed)** and **anxiously**.*
- *underline every reference to **those God is speaking to** and **those who fear the Lord**. Watch carefully for pronouns.*

DISCUSS

- What were God's instructions to His people in Isaiah 41:10? What reason did He give?

- How would the promise of Isaiah 41:10 help you in the fears of life?

- Besides living it out, how could you use this verse to help others when they go through difficulties?

- What did you learn in Malachi from marking the references to those who fear the Lord and esteem His name?

- What do you think it means to esteem the name of the Lord? Would it have any connection with fearing the Lord? Explain your answer.

that I prepare My own possession, and I will spare them as a man spares his own son who serves him."

18 So you will again distinguish between the righteous and the wicked, between one who serves God and one who does not serve Him.

4:1 "For behold, the day is coming, burning like a furnace; and all the arrogant and every evildoer will be chaff; and the day that is coming will set them ablaze," says the LORD of hosts, "so that it will leave them neither root nor branch."

2 "But for you who fear My name, the sun of righteousness will rise

with healing in its wings; and you will go forth and skip about like calves from the stall.

3 "You will tread down the wicked, for they will be ashes under the soles of your feet on the day which I am preparing," says the LORD of hosts.

• Malachi, the last book of the Old Testament, is a post-exile book, which means it was written after Israel was restored from captivity. What insight do you get from these verses into the future? What are God's plans for and promises to His people?

ECCLESIASTES 12:13–14

13 The conclusion, when all has been heard, is: fear God and keep His commandments, because this applies to every person.

14 For God will bring every act to judgment, everything which is hidden, whether it is good or evil.

OBSERVE

So what is the bottom line of all you've learned in this study?

Leader: Read Ecclesiastes 12:13–14 aloud with the group. Then have the group...
   • *draw a triangle over every reference to* **God.**
   • *draw a jagged circle around the phrase* **fear God.**

DISCUSS

• Who is to fear God and keep His commandments?

• Why?

• What do you think would happen in your nation if people began to understand all you've learned about the fear of the Lord? What areas of darkness might it dispel?

• When you look at our society, do you really think people need to fear God, to know Him so they can be what God created them to be—and know His peace?

• If you fear God what is your responsibility in this? Why don't you pray that God will lead you to someone who needs to hear what you've learned about the fear of the Lord.

WRAP IT UP

The Bible tells us that "by the word of the LORD the heavens were made…. He spoke, and it was done" (Psalm 33:6, 9). Therefore, "let all the earth fear the LORD; let all the inhabitants of the world stand in awe of Him" (Psalm 33:8).

But they don't, do they?

And because people don't know or fear their Creator, because they don't honor God as God, there is conflict on the face of the earth. The continued rejection of the evidence and knowledge of God brings mankind into increasing darkness. With that darkness, fear intensifies.

Darkness is the womb from which fear is born. Yet in God there is no darkness at all; God is light. And God is love. And so because of the great love with which God loves us, God gives to man His Son, the Word in human flesh, the light of life so we can see for ourselves what it is to fear the Lord.

Isaiah wrote it, Jesus fulfilled it: "The Spirit of the LORD will rest on Him, the spirit of wisdom and understanding, the spirit of counsel and strength, the spirit of knowledge and the fear of the LORD. And He will delight in the fear of the LORD" (11:2–3).

To walk in the fear of the Lord is to live as Jesus lived, doing nothing on our own initiative, obeying God's words, doing His works. To fear the Lord, to trust Him. To respect Him, believing that God is who He says He is and that He will do what He says He will do. Remember what we read in Isaiah 50:10: "Who among you fears the LORD and obeys the voice of his servant? Let him who walks in darkness and has no light trust in the name of the LORD and rely on his God" (ESV).

You've seen for yourself that the fear the Lord is the beginning of knowledge and of wisdom. It frees us from the grip of all lesser fears and paves the way for success, just as God promised Joshua. Success comes through being strong and courageous so that the fear of God keeps you from turning to the right or the left; instead you keep to the narrow straight way that leads to eternal life. Fear of the Lord comes from learning God's Word, meditating on it and letting it go so deep into the fiber of your being that you are compelled to live by it. Fear that causes you to do all He commands:

The precepts of the LORD are right, rejoicing the heart;
The commandment of the LORD is pure, enlightening the eyes.
The fear of the LORD is clean, enduring forever;
The judgments of the LORD are true; they are righteous altogether.
They are more desirable than gold, yes, than much fine gold;
Sweeter also than honey and the drippings of the honeycomb.
Moreover, by them Your servant is warned;
In keeping them there is great reward. (Psalm 19:8–11)

Here is the answer to breaking free from the fears that hold you back: "The secret of the LORD is for those who fear Him" (Psalm 25:14).

This is the fear that conquers all fear.

40 MINUTE BIBLE STUDIES

No-Homework
That Help You

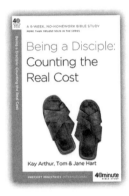

A 6-WEEK, NO-HOMEWORK BIBLE STUDY
MORE THAN 700,000 SOLD IN THE SERIES

Being a Disciple:
Counting the
Real Cost

Kay Arthur, Tom & Jane Hart

PRECEPT MINISTRIES INTERNATIONAL

40minute BIBLE STUDY

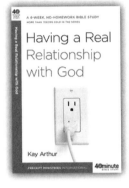

A 6-WEEK, NO-HOMEWORK BIBLE STUDY
MORE THAN 700,000 SOLD IN THE SERIES

Having a Real
Relationship
with God

Kay Arthur

PRECEPT MINISTRIES INTERNATIONAL

40minute BIBLE STUDY

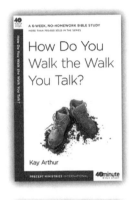

A 6-WEEK, NO-HOMEWORK BIBLE STUDY
MORE THAN 700,000 SOLD IN THE SERIES

How Do You
Walk the Walk
You Talk?

Kay Arthur

PRECEPT MINISTRIES INTERNATIONAL

40minute BIBLE STUDY

A 6-WEEK, NO-HOMEWORK BIBLE STUDY
MORE THAN 700,000 SOLD IN THE SERIES

Living a
Life of
True Worship

Kay Arthur, Bob & Diane Vereen

PRECEPT MINISTRIES INTERNATIONAL

40minute BIBLE STUDY

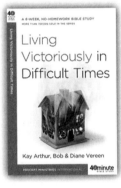

A 6-WEEK, NO-HOMEWORK BIBLE STUDY
MORE THAN 700,000 SOLD IN THE SERIES

Living
Victoriously in
Difficult Times

Kay Arthur, Bob & Diane Vereen

PRECEPT MINISTRIES INTERNATIONAL

40minute BIBLE STUDY

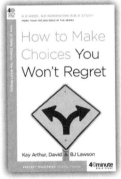

A 6-WEEK, NO-HOMEWORK BIBLE STUDY
MORE THAN 700,000 SOLD IN THE SERIES

How to Make
Choices You
Won't Regret

Kay Arthur, David & BJ Lawson

40minute BIBLE STUDY

A 6-WEEK, NO-HOMEWORK BIBLE STUDY
MORE THAN 700,000 SOLD IN THE SERIES

Money and
Possessions:
The Quest for
Contentment

Kay Arthur & David Arthur

PRECEPT MINISTRIES INTERNATIONAL

40minute BIBLE STUDY

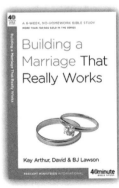

A 6-WEEK, NO-HOMEWORK BIBLE STUDY
MORE THAN 700,000 SOLD IN THE SERIES

Building a
Marriage That
Really Works

Kay Arthur, David & BJ Lawson

PRECEPT MINISTRIES INTERNATIONAL

40minute BIBLE STUDY

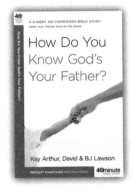

A 6-WEEK, NO-HOMEWORK BIBLE STUDY
MORE THAN 700,000 SOLD IN THE SERIES

How Do You
Know God's
Your Father?

Kay Arthur, David & BJ Lawson

PRECEPT MINISTRIES INTERNATIONAL

40minute BIBLE STUDY

Bible Studies
Discover Truth For Yourself

Discovering What the Future Holds

Kay Arthur & Georg Huber

Forgiveness: Breaking the Power of the Past

Kay Arthur, David & BJ Lawson

Living Like You Belong to God

Kay Arthur, David & BJ Lawson

The Essentials of Effective Prayer

Kay Arthur, David & BJ Lawson

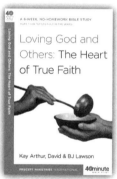

Loving God and Others: The Heart of True Faith

Kay Arthur, David & BJ Lawson

Understanding Spiritual Gifts

Kay Arthur, David and BJ Lawson

Also Available:
A Man's Strategy for Conquering Temptation
Rising to the Call of Leadership
Key Principles of Biblical Fasting
What Does the Bible Say About Sex?
Turning Your Heart Toward God
Fatal Distractions: Conquering Destructive Temptations
Spiritual Warfare: Overcoming the Enemy
The Power of Knowing God
Breaking Free from Fear

Another powerful study series
from beloved Bible teacher

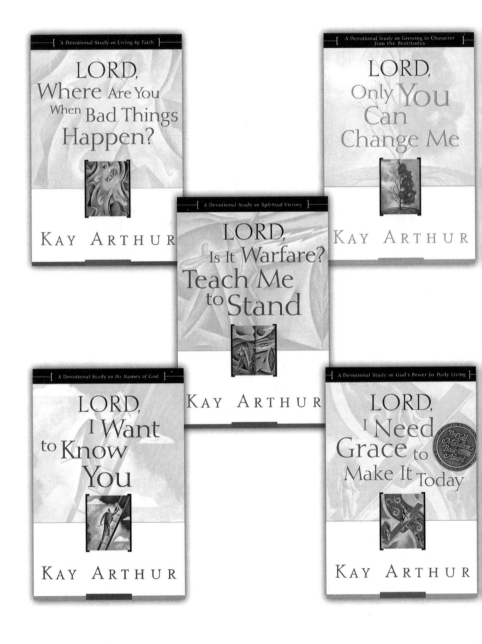

[A Devotional Study on Living by Faith]

LORD,
Where Are You
When Bad Things
Happen?

KAY ARTHUR

[A Devotional Study on Growing in Character
from the Beatitudes]

LORD,
Only You
Can
Change Me

KAY ARTHUR

[A Devotional Study on Spiritual Victory]

LORD,
Is It Warfare?
Teach Me
to Stand

KAY ARTHUR

[A Devotional Study on the Names of God]

LORD,
I Want
to Know
You

KAY ARTHUR

[A Devotional Study on God's Power for Daily Living]

LORD,
I Need
Grace to
Make It Today

KAY ARTHUR

KAY ARTHUR

The Lord series provides insightful, warm-hearted Bible studies designed to meet you where you are—and help you discover God's answers to your deepest needs.

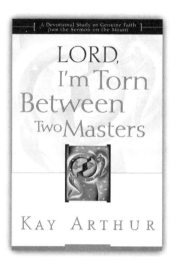

[A Devotional Study on Genuine Faith from the Sermon on the Mount]

LORD, I'm Torn Between Two Masters

KAY ARTHUR

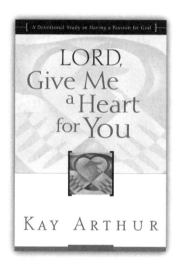

[A Devotional Study on Having a Passion for God]

LORD, Give Me a Heart for You

KAY ARTHUR

[A Devotional Study on God's Care and Deliverance]

LORD, Heal My Hurts

KAY ARTHUR

ALSO AVAILABLE:
One-year devotionals to draw you closer to the heart of God.

366 Appointments with God

Lord, I Give You This Day

KAY ARTHUR

Appointments With God

SEARCH MY HEART, O GOD

KAY ARTHUR

KAY ARTHUR is known around the world as an international Bible teacher, author, conference speaker, and host of the national radio and television programs *Precepts for Life,* which reaches a worldwide viewing audience of over 94 million. A four-time Gold Medallion Award–winning author, Kay has authored more than 100 books and Bible studies.

Kay and her husband, Jack, founded Precept Ministries International in 1970 in Chattanooga, Tennessee, with a vision to establish people in God's Word. Today, the ministry has a worldwide outreach. In addition to inductive study training workshops and thousands of small-group studies across America, PMI reaches nearly 150 countries with inductive Bible studies translated into nearly 70 languages, teaching people to discover Truth for themselves.

Contact Precept Ministries International for more information about inductive Bible studies in your area.

Precept Ministries International
PO Box 182218
Chattanooga, TN 37422-7218
800-763-8280
www.precept.org